TRICIA GUILD
DECORATING WITH
COLOR

MERE COLOR, UNSPOILED BY MEANING,
AND UNALLIED WITH DEFINITE FORM,
CAN SPEAK TO THE SOUL IN A
THOUSAND DIFFERENT WAYS.

OSCAR WILDE

FOR MERYL, WHO SENSES EVERY SHADE

TRICIA GUILD
DECORATING WITH
COLOR

PHOTOGRAPHY BY JAMES MERRELL

TEXT BY AMANDA BACK WITH TRICIA GUILD

RIZZOLI
NEW YORK

New York · Paris · London · Milan

CONTENTS

LIVING IN COLOR

For as long as I can remember, color has played a vital role in my life. Choosing colors, as well as living and working with them, has always been a matter of personal expression and one that, for me, is instinctive and often spontaneous. Much of the way that I work with color depends on my immediate response and reaction to a particular shade or group of colors—how they make my heart sing or beat a little faster is the only science that I use. My personal form of expression is visual; my language of choice is articulated by the various elements I use in an interior to convey my particular style. I believe the rooms and spaces that I create in my work speak for themselves and demonstrate instantly how color can enrich and invigorate our lives.

Choosing color is by its very nature intrinsically personal and subjective; it can also be an intensely stimulating experience. There is an energy and a mood that surrounds every tone and shade of each color with which, at some primal level, we make a connection when we make our choices; a connection that, ultimately, says something about who we are, what we love, and how we want to live.

Tastes and attitudes shift and change with time; so, too, the range of colors I use evolves, but it is not only the shade and tone of individual colors that is important. I am known for my use of strong, confident tones, but in my opinion what makes them work is the way these are carefully balanced with whites and naturals. I have always been a passionate believer in the ability of these clear colors to control strength and provide a harmonious note. In the same way, print and decorative pattern have always played an important role in what I do, yet calm expanses of plain textures are as vital to the mix as those that are richly patterned.

Vital though color is in its pure form, it is just one of several components in my particular artist's palette. While it is not the only ingredient that can make an interior work, color is without doubt, the best place to start. Architecture, light, texture, and pattern each play their part in ensuring that a room not only looks beautiful but serves its purpose and evokes the desired mood and spirit. But when combined with color the permutations are almost endless. Consider, for example, how the gauzy dreaminess of a turquoise linen voile at a summery window looks and feels quite different from the rich intensity of a turquoise velvet sofa in a formal drawing room.

Inevitably, it is the balance between these different elements that gives an interior personality and life. It is that particular alchemical blend of color reacting with texture, pattern, and light that can ultimately lead to some sort of magic, creating a space where we feel at home and where we can be true to ourselves.

On the pages that follow, I have tried to dissect my own instinctive response to the colors that I love and am currently using, in the hope that you too can find your own sense of color and enjoy expressing it as much as I do.

COLOR IS A JOYFUL AND INSTINCTIVE PLEASURE LIFE ENHANCING ROMANTIC MAGICAL

TRICIA GUILD

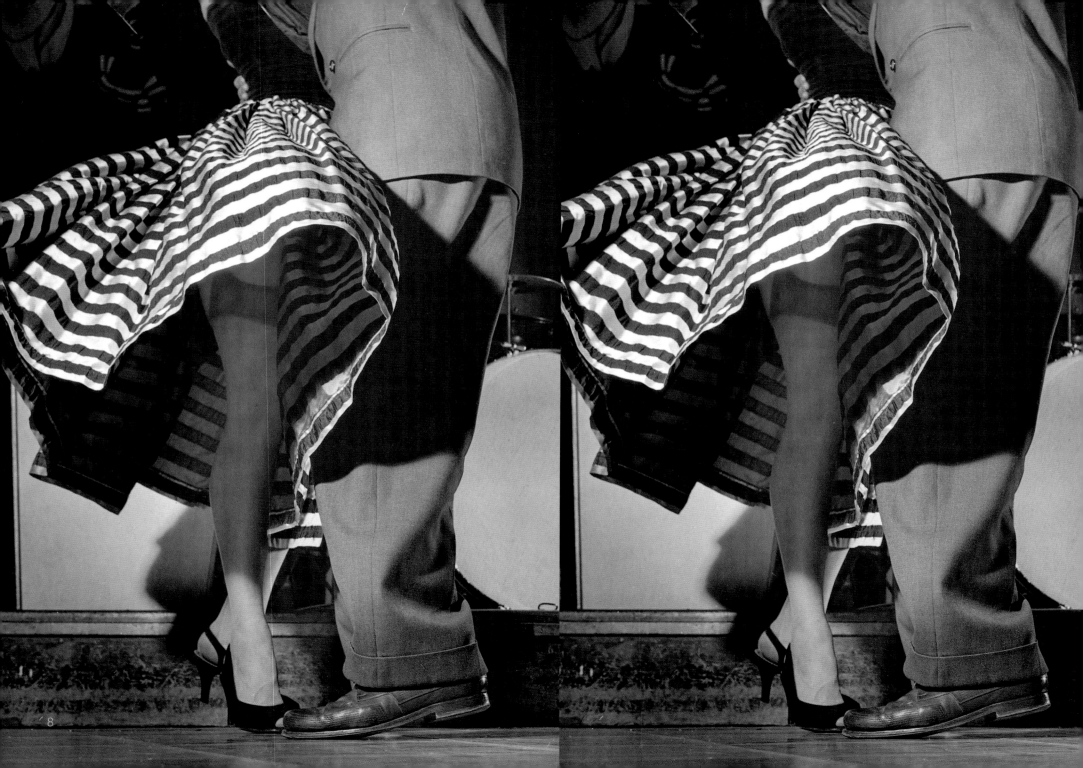

The combination of black and white is as timeless as it is definitive. Just as the polar opposites of night and day or north and south are inextricably linked together, black and white form a never-ending partnership that intersperses our style and taste with simplicity, classicism and, often, an incisive edge. This dynamic duo is a signature of formality and gravitas; almost without us knowing, it forms the backbone to a world of color.

The photographer Ted Grant once said: "When you photograph people in color, you photograph their clothes. But when you photograph people in black and white, you photograph their souls." It is that incisive, almost primal notion that lies at the heart of monochrome. It is not for nothing that when we seek the truth, we ask for it in black and white—in its simplest, plainest terms. The effect of black and white together can be as conflicting as the colors themselves: sometimes nostalgic and classic but just as easily modern and contemporary, serious and authoritative as well as flippant and flirtatious. Dynamic and strong, or as romantic as an old movie, monochrome can sharpen a room and add a timeless focus.

Halfway between the two lies the color gray, the forceful gravitas of black lightened with the purity and innocence of white. Gray is often seen as an intellectual and considered color, but may also be accused of being somber and pessimistic, nondescript and bland. To assume this is all the color has to offer is to ignore its potential for elegance, serenity, understatement, and calm. The renowned Danish artist Vilhelm Hammershøi's poetic paintings and portraits are known for a strict palette of muted grays and neutrals—their atmosphere of stillness and calm is only made possible by the coolness of its lead grays and cloudy charcoals.

In the following pages we view interiors of black and white and gray in a variety of guises, from sharp tailoring to romantic nostalgia, from the backdrop to a riot of color to a quiet stillness. Uniting them all is that graphic edge that, like the lead in our pencils, is simplicity itself.

The artist's studio on pages 12–13 belongs to one of Britain's most prominent artists, Howard Hodgkin. Known for the vibrant, emotional, and intoxicating strokes of rich color in his paintings, those same brushstrokes resonate with a timeless purity when condensed to a monochrome palette. His fabrics for Designers Guild were recently relaunched after twenty-five years and their intrinsic power is as great now as it was then.

Shades of black and white in the bedroom suite on pages 16–17 evoke the romantic nostalgia of a classic black-and-white movie. With its encaustic tiled floors, the room already has a sense of classicism. One wall is papered with a pattern of exuberant bouquets of flowers—almost like a photograph, the flowers are finely picked out in delicate shades of cloudy, watery charcoals. The strict repetition of the pattern harnesses the exuberance of the flowers. The same pattern hangs at the French windows but partnered with a tailored linen stripe of graphite and white. The bed is dressed with a casual, tumbled mass of white linen, which gives the monochrome breathing space and an expanse of purity. A small upholstered bench is covered in a lush silvery velvet echoing the tones of the flowered walls, while a glossy silky pillow of graphite and silver is given further impact with monochrome stripes, reminding us that for all the romance, the room is not weak or overtly feminine but relaxed and confident.

In the living room on pages 22–23, a checkerboard of black-and-white tiles forms the starting point for the decoration. The inherent strength of the crisp, monochrome color palette stands up to the grand architecture and the textures and pattern used soften any hard edges, creating a dancing, joyful room that is classic, timeless, yet full of life. The walls are covered in an almost botanical, organic print of topiary trees, finely etched in charcoal on a white vellum ground. At a pair of tall windows hang unlined translucent banners of the same design as well as banners of washed linen stripes in graphic black and white. An elegant trim of glossy black leaves adds definition and focus to the windows. While the palette remains clipped, the furniture in the room is covered in a mix of linen stripes of varying sizes, playing with the scale but keeping the room uniform in its simplicity.

The stylish hallway on pages 24–25 is a study in restraint: a palette of duck-egg blue, icy white, and dove gray immediately creates a mood of refined tranquility. The washed, tumbled linen banners feature enormous peony heads of Gustavian gray blue—the scale is unexpected and dramatic and adds impact to the restful quality of the space. The same large flower covers the back of an elegant bergère and softly washed ice-blue velvet covers the seat. The elements of scale and texture add interest and touches of unexpected eccentricity while the sinuous curves of the bannisters and the lights in dark graphite add a layer of strength to the stillness.

The mood in the conservatory on pages 28–29 is one of relaxed sophistication. The walls are painted a fresh cool white while the ornate moldings and multipaned doors leading to the room behind are picked out in a lead gray; a blond wooden floor adds to the neutral scheme. The main conservatory is a study of cool neutrality while the walls of the anteroom, which are visible from the conservatory, are papered in a design of tonal flowers—chalky gray, celadon, and dusky mauve roses tumble across the walls giving hints of color while respecting the stillness of the atmosphere. A generous sofa in steel–gray washed linen is the focal point of the room. Casually strewn with pillows of natural linens and tumbled cottons, it positively invites the visitor to relax. Soft celadon colors different objects in the room from a linen pillow to ceramics and vases on the vintage table. A mix of contemporary and vintage furniture gives the room a gentle nudge of modernity while the patterned roses in the distance convey the sense of comfort and restraint.

In the suite of rooms on pages 30–33 a soft dove gray is the main player while darkly inky black and white give flashes of life and vitality. In both rooms the walls are covered with a shimmery pearl-gray paper. The same design is used to cover the base of the formal sofa but in a darker color, immediately giving the room a note of strength. The seats of the sofa are covered in contrasting silvery velvet, adding a touch of softness. A pair of tailored chairs sit opposite, one in a dark charcoal velvet, the other in the same design as the walls and sofa but darker still. The different tones shift the balance of the room adding interest and impact. The furniture is grouped around a contrasting pair of rugs—one a creamy silk, the other a more graphic pattern of black on white, which adds another layer of strength and heralds the cascading flowers at the windows of the room beyond. Here silver and graphite flowers tumble on natural linen in a serene study of intensity. The strength of the room is further underlined by the striking grouping of a collection of pictures and photographs to one side of the architrave, giving the room an unexpected eccentricity that arrests the formality and adds vitality. The trio of glowing orange lampshades provides a sudden jolt of color and heat that stops the room from being subdued and allows its character to shine.

Black, white, and silvery gray are the backdrop for strong vital colors and grand-scale pattern in the hallway on pages 34–35. The floors are black-and-stone checkerboard; denoting a sense of classic formality. A series of windows are hung with large panels of colorful, vivacious flowers on either soft gray or moody charcoal grounds. The sheer exuberance of the flowers and the scale of the design are reined in by a subtle use of monochrome: black-and-white silk stripes edge every panel and echo the classic floor, pulling the scheme together.

BLACK
GUNMETAL
GRAPHITE
GRAY
CHALK
RAVEN
SLATE
CHARCOAL

THE ONLY WAY AN ARTIST CAN COMMUNICATE
WITH THE WORLD AT LARGE IS ON THE
LEVEL OF FEELING.   HOWARD HODGKIN

13

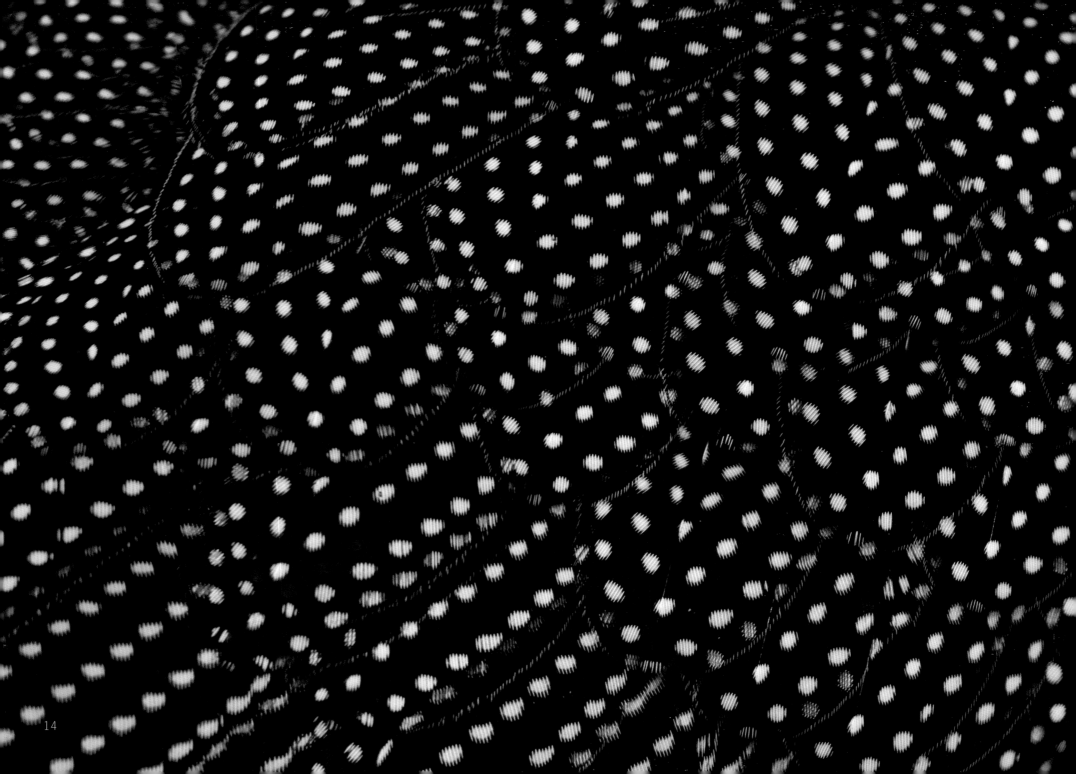

ALWAYS
DYNAMIC
NEVER OUT OF
FASHION
BLACK
A N D
WHITE
MAKES
EVERYTHING
ELSE LOOK BETTER

SUBTLE
RESTFUL
TONE ON TONE
HARMONIOUS
GRAYS
AND
EARTH
SHADES
BALANCE
BRIGHT COLOR

VIVID
SURPRISING
A SUDDEN JOLT
OF PURE BRIGHT
COLOR
A D D S
DRAMA
ACCENT
UNEXPECTED
SOPHISTICATION

31

BLACK IS A FORCE: I DEPEND
ON BLACK TO SIMPLIFY THE
CONSTRUCTION.   HENRI MATISSE

More people claim blue as their favorite color than any other. What is it that makes blue so universally loved—is it the soaring optimism of the endless blue skies that it symbolizes, or the calm, expansive freedom of the ocean, or perhaps its pensive purity that evokes such strong feelings in many of us?

The power of blue has been recognized for thousands of years: to the ancient Egyptians lapis lazuli was the sacred stone of the gods; to the Aztecs, blue was the color of nobility and strength; the delicate forms of the Ming and Qing porcelain dynasties from the first century in China nearly always featured cobalt blue. The dye prepared from the Indian plant Indigofera tinctoria gave us the deep inky-dark beauty of indigo, brought to Europe by Marco Polo in the thirteenth century. Nowadays, blue's familiar, feel-good qualities color all aspects of our lives—from the blue of our denim jeans to the blue ink in our pens to classic, blue and white pottery.

Its role in decorating has not always been as straightforward, however. Many consider it a cold and difficult color to use, yet the simplicity of a blue and white room is a timeless statement. Blue in all its many guises offers a variety of different styles from dramatic to ethereal, from crisp utilitarian to a lavish richness. The rooms in the following pages depict a variety of architectural styles, yet the use of blue throughout confirms its versatility.

The hallway on pages 40–41 shows rich cobalt blue in all its intensity. The old, rather heavy wooden staircase and the carved wooden moldings and lintels needed a color to complement their inherent strength. A vibrant, cobalt blue flocked velvet wallpaper brings the space to life and stands up to the architecture's intensity. Had a less intense shade been used, the hallway might have seemed a little old-fashioned, but the bold, rich hue works with the wood, the velvet textures softening the hard edges to create a space of dramatic power. A small vintage chair covered in two fabrics, both an inky velvet and a more robust linen chenille, adds to the sense of drama while playing with the scale of the space and giving an unexpected hint of modernity.

The hallway leads on to a smaller anteroom (pages 42–43) where the strong architectural theme continues. Here, the ornate doors and lintels are painted a soft dove gray. The brilliance of blue is carried through to this suite of rooms, where a softly shaded wallpaper graduates vertically from deepest indigo through cobalt and kingfisher and eventually to white, enhancing the space and working with the architecture to take your eye upward, creating an

ethereal, uplifting sense of space. Informal chairs covered in washed linen echo the crisp scheme but add a more decorative note; a pile of pillows add to the air of relaxed formality.

The anteroom leads through to a larger, slightly more formal living room on pages 44–45. The scale of the room, as well as its architectural detailing, requires an equally compelling scheme, and here indigo and white strike a powerful yet effortless note. The shaded design used on the walls in the anteroom reappears on simple unlined linen drapes. The floor is layered with rugs in strong geometric designs that anchor the space. A generous sofa is covered in heavy, luxurious indigo linen and pillows in washed white linen add an inviting sense of relaxation and comfort. Unlined muslin drapes hang at the tall windows behind the sofa, the classical print of the drapes respectfully echoing the traditional proportions of the room while more relaxed white linen banners underline the air of casual calm. The color palette is purposely kept tight and so remains strong; the textures bring the room to life and add modernity and serenity.

The purity of blue and white takes on another character in the apartment featured on pages 46–49. Once more the architecture provides the starting point with its intricate encaustic tiled floor. As well as natural shades of terracotta, stone, and charcoal, a vivid blue adds color to the antique floor and it is this cerulean blue that forms the basis of the scheme for the entire suite of rooms.

In the living room, two walls are painted bright white and one is papered in a geometric design using two tones of blue. The graphic quality of the wall provides a strong statement from which the rest of the room flows. Tailored, masculine felted wool covers a sweeping sofa, giving the room a dignified focus. A pair of matching armchairs is covered in the same striped wool and a different geometric velvet in charcoal and cerulean reflects the complexity of the floor and works with it rather than fighting it. Striped silk pillows introduce a note of glossy black, adding depth and luxury, while at the adjoining window a heavy cotton drape is printed with wide bands of intricate mosaic patterns in shades of cobalt and chalk that echo the pattern of the tiled floor. The smart, tailored textures and the darker tones of charcoal give this blue room strength and character.

On page 50 an outdoor summer table is swathed in a wonderful cloth of azure blue tie-dyed linen. Set against the natural stone of the terrace clad in lush ivy and acacia, the vintage café chairs each have a pillow of washed linen in shades of turquoise, pewter, and indigo, providing a cool and inviting place to have an alfresco lunch. Leading in from the backyard is a large morning room (pages 52–53) where the same tie-dyed indigo is used as a drape at one of the elegant windows. The hand-dyed fabric is matched at the other window by softly shaded linen, each providing a sharp accent of color against the otherwise neutral interior.

In the study shown on pages 54–57 one wall is papered with a decorative, almost chinoiserie floral print, picking up the blue in the floor. A small curvy bench is covered in a watery blue, striped velvet. Pillows on the sofa introduce a new palette of turquoise, lime, and magenta, which also covers a pair of small chairs, the mix different for each, yet working harmoniously within the room. Blue and white is the canvas from which other colors and details give the room its vitality.

A small breakfast room on pages 60–61 shows how shades of blue, from the softest sky to deepest cobalt, can work together to create a joyful, simple mix. Elegant silvery blue silk hangs at the window, decorated with flowers and exotic birds in cobalt, teal, and white. A banner of cobalt and white stripes hangs next to it adding a stroke of modernity and almost controlling the elegance. The pattern is further reined in by the group of chairs gathered around the dining table, covered in expanses of plain washed linen in the same tones of cobalt, teal, and white with the odd accent of stripe. They give the room an unexpected note and prove that blue and white, while a classic combination, need never be boring.

The last two rooms in this chapter, on pages 62–67, show a much softer side of blue and an altogether different mood. Here, the chalky walls of the architecture and pale terracotta floors need a softer touch. A large-scale floral print in shades of pewter and delft covers one wall and hangs in heavy linen swathes at the window. The floor is layered with rugs in shades of pewter, ocean, and chalk, giving a sense of calm purity. Smooth sofas are covered in chalky white linen and the seats in a houndstooth check of dove gray and porcelain blue. One strong cobalt drape hangs at the window picking up the stronger blue of a rug and giving the room a stroke of dynamism and modernity. The ethereal, romantic mood is carried through to the adjoining hallway, where the soft blue is used with black, adding a graphic touch, yet the space remains entirely calm and serene. Sinuous, curved sofas are covered in striking velvet animal print and scattered with pillows in washed linens; the luxurious textures provide the perfect contrast to the hard floors and stone walls.

BLUE
COBALT
LAPIS LAZULI
INDIGO
FORGET-ME-NOT
IRIS
AZURE
DELPHINIUM

COBALT IS A DIVINE COLOR
AND THERE IS NOTHING AS
FINE FOR PUTTING AN
ATMOSPHERE ROUND THINGS.
VINCENT VAN GOGH

43

THERE ARE CONNOISSEURS OF BLUE JUST AS THERE ARE CONNOISSEURS OF WINE.   COLETTE

BLUE IS THE ONLY COLOR WHICH MAINTAINS ITS OWN CHARACTER IN ALL ITS TONES. TAKE BLUE IN ALL ITS NUANCES, FROM THE DARKEST TO THE LIGHTEST —IT WILL ALWAYS STAY BLUE.

RAOUL DUFY

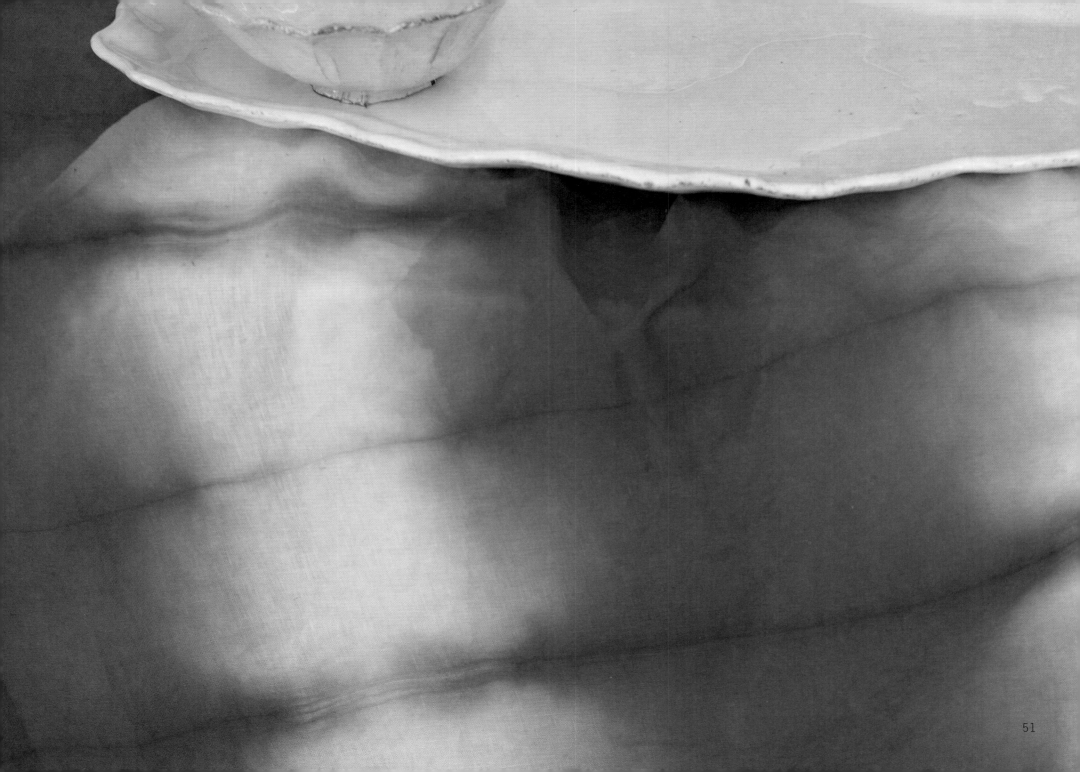

CLEAR BLUE SKIES

WHITE CLOUDS

CLEAR

HEAVENLY

BLUE

VIBRANT

PERFECT

FORGET-ME-NOT

BEAUTIFUL

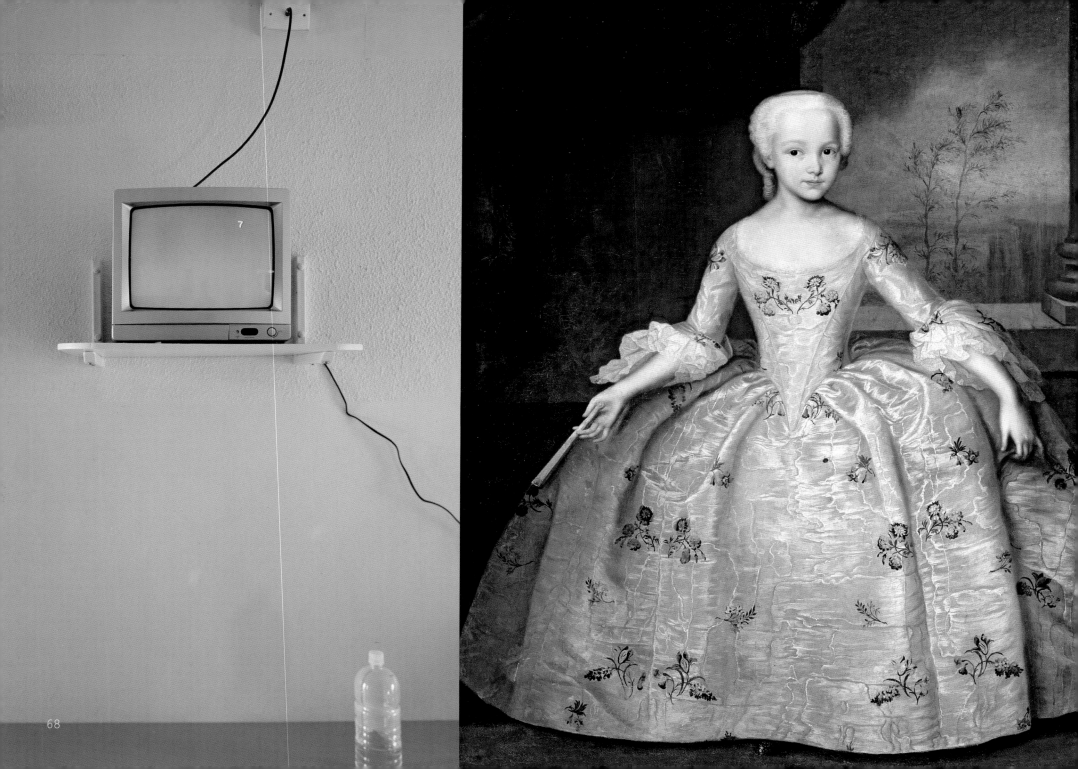

Somewhere between the lush vitality of green and the dreamy intensity of blue lies a group of colors whose presence is altogether more mysterious and harder to define than either of their primary sources. Uplifting, enduring, calm, and always elegant, these clear, harmonious tones have the ability to work with both warm and cool colors, inevitably adding a dash of their ethereal beauty to the mix. Some of them take their names from precious stones: turquoise, jade, and aquamarine have all been used for centuries to symbolize wealth and spirituality. In Persian, turquoise is known as "ferozah," meaning "victorious," and the ancient Persians used tiles of pure turquoise to cover the domes of temples and palaces to symbolize heaven on earth. Turquoise has also adorned the ceremonial costumes and crowns of rulers and leaders of a great many noble civilizations. In China, as early as 6,000 BCE, jade was considered the imperial gem and it was often intricately carved into precious objects. Its heavenly, ethereal qualities are still as highly prized in the Far East today. Other tones in this serene group take their names and inspiration from the fresh watery elements that they conjure up: ocean, sea spray, aqua, sea foam, and glass evoke a crystal-clear delicacy that is as timeless as the oceans themselves. And indeed the color of a pane of glass, when viewed sideways, is that particular shiny pale green that is almost indefinable and definitely not present when one views the surface of the window. It is that barely there, dreamy quality that these colors can evoke.

When used in interiors, these colors are incredibly versatile, either providing a cool and serene backdrop or that unexpected dash of color when needed. Discover their versatility in the following pages, from the dazzling, almost primal intensity of pure turquoise through to the barely there delicacy of eau de nil and sea spray, they are all united by an insouciant glassy beauty.

On pages 74–79, a clear and vivid palette of lettuce green, turquoise, and sea glass forms the basis of a scheme for the open plan living area of a contemporary family home. Here the mood is modern and crisp, taking its cue from the uncompromising contemporary architecture. Concrete floors and walls of glass doors flood the space with light, which is filtered with banners of shaded linen that

fades from turquoise to sea glass. In this space, texture is everything; curvy white chairs are grouped around a smooth concrete table in alabaster, while at the other end of the room a large modular sofa of white leather provides a natural ending. A rich, deep turquoise rug gives the room a strong focal point, while an ottoman of beech wood and pure white linen holds piles of pillows in soft jade and pale aqua and a decorative throw of emerald and turquoise. An undulating vintage sofa is covered in snake–print velvet, in palest aqua, with one large, flowered pillow giving the space a patterned note that adds vitality to the cool, plain textures. Transparent curvy glass vases in sea green and sea glass further accentuate the floating sense of calm. The natural elements of glass and stone, wood and concrete are enhanced with a dreamy mix of plain, cool washes of color that reflect the light and infuse the space with their sparkling freshness.

An antique fireplace was the starting point for the bedroom scheme on pages 80–81. Intricately laid with ancient Portuguese Azulejos tiles of deep turquoise and eau de nil with touches of citrus yellow, the chimney breast sets the tone for the room. Just as the tiles fade from dark to light, the walls are covered with a shaded paper that starts at turquoise then fades through ocean and ultimately to white. A silky, shaded rug in the same tones contrasts with the raw wooden floors and adds a touch of shiny luxury to the room. The windows are dressed with sheer linen banners in contrasting designs: one of painterly yellow flowers, the other the same shaded turquoise as the walls—the cool aqua filters the sunlight, giving the room a calm and ethereal sense of stillness that matches the intensity of the fireplace yet allows the room to breathe.

The morning room on pages 84–85 shows pale jade in a contemplative yet slightly eclectic mood. The walls are covered in a shaded paper, starting with a deep jade at the base and fading upward through pale aqua to eau de nil. The striking black-and-white floor adds to the classical spirit of the space and a vintage Bertoia armchair, covered in a jade snake-print velvet with charcoal accents, gives the room a strong focal point. A rug in the same tones relates back to the walls while the tall, elegant doors that open onto the backyard are hung with a casual fall of tie-dyed linen in jade and alabaster. Subtle notes of charcoal in the room balance the jade and the almost nonchalant mix of textures, pattern, and plains evokes a dreamy elegance that is both timeless and coolly laid back.

The formal living room on pages 86–89 demonstrates how jade and aqua can work as part of a team to create a scheme of vitality and depth. The scale of the room demands a note of strength but one that does not overpower or dominate. Panels to dado height are painted in a rich charcoal while the walls above are papered in an intricate large-scale print of pencil-drawn urns and flowers in tones of sepia and travertine highlighted with chartreuse and softest ocean. A pair of generous angular sofas face each other over a large-scale striped rug of citrus, sepia, and turquoise that grounds the room. One sofa is covered in washed velvet stripes of natural, turquoise, and faded indigo, while the other provides a jolt of color in a sharp citrine velvet. Both sofas are decorated with pillows of varying sizes and textures in plain ocean blue, alabaster, and lime. The same zingy yellow of the sofa colors a silk banner at the windows, which is just visible from behind a more formal silk of printed urns and flowers. Turquoise and aqua give the room a sense of calm and serenity; the accompanying zesty citrus adds a note of wit and vitality, making the room sing yet respecting its classical proportions and architecture.

Shades of aqua and jade give the morning room on pages 92–93 a reflective yet contemporary feel. The neutral stone walls and cool black-and-white tiled floor form the blank canvas. A crisp linen decorated with beautifully drawn and painted vases and flowers hangs at the tall French windows; the studied nature of the print immediately captures a mood of stillness and ethereal calm. Hanging at the other side of the window is a simple shaded linen, its tones of deep jade to aqua and white capturing the different tones and nuances of the patterned banner, its textured plainness adding a note of strength. A generous modern sofa covered in snake-print velvet, in tones of jade and charcoal, adds further strength, while pillows of the same ombré linen at the window pull the scheme together. The whimsical charm of the print is offset by the shaded linen and the snake print. In much the same way, the charcoal gives dreamy aqua a note of powerful intensity.

AQUA
TURQUOISE
CERULEAN
OCEAN
EAU DE NIL
JADE
MARINE
DUCK-EGG BLUE

LEARN TO SEE AND TO FEEL LIFE ... CULTIVATE IMAGINATION, BECAUSE THERE ARE STILL MARVELS

IN THE WORLD, BECAUSE LIFE IS A MYSTERY AND ALWAYS WILL BE, BUT BE AWARE OF IT.

JOSEF ALBERS

COLOR IS JOY. ONE DOES NOT THINK JOY. ONE IS CARRIED BY IT.
ERNST HAAS

80

WHY DO TWO COLORS, PUT ONE NEXT TO THE OTHER,
SING? CAN ONE REALLY EXPLAIN THIS? NO.
JUST AS ONE CAN NEVER LEARN HOW TO PAINT.
PABLO PICASSO

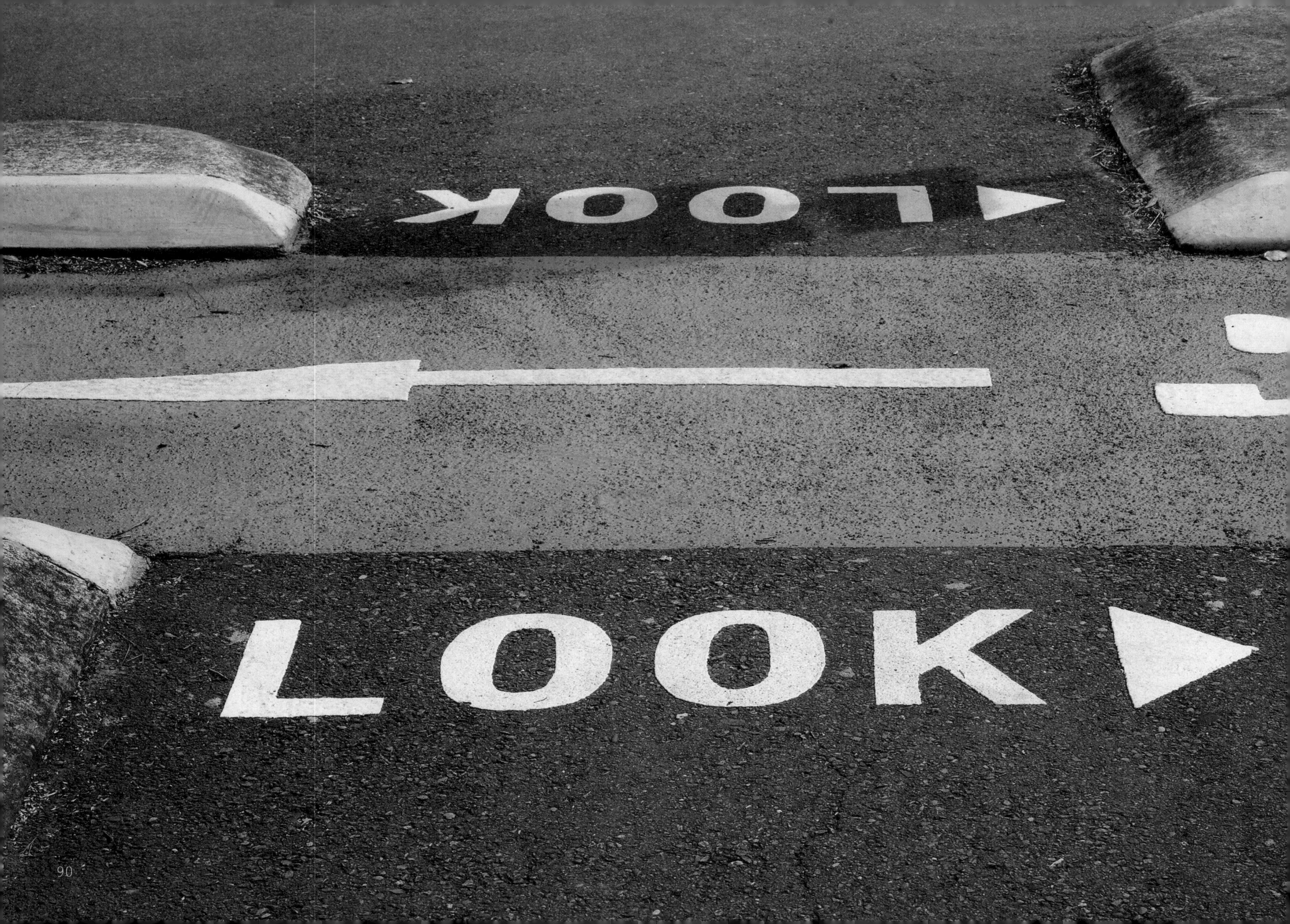
LOOK
LOOK

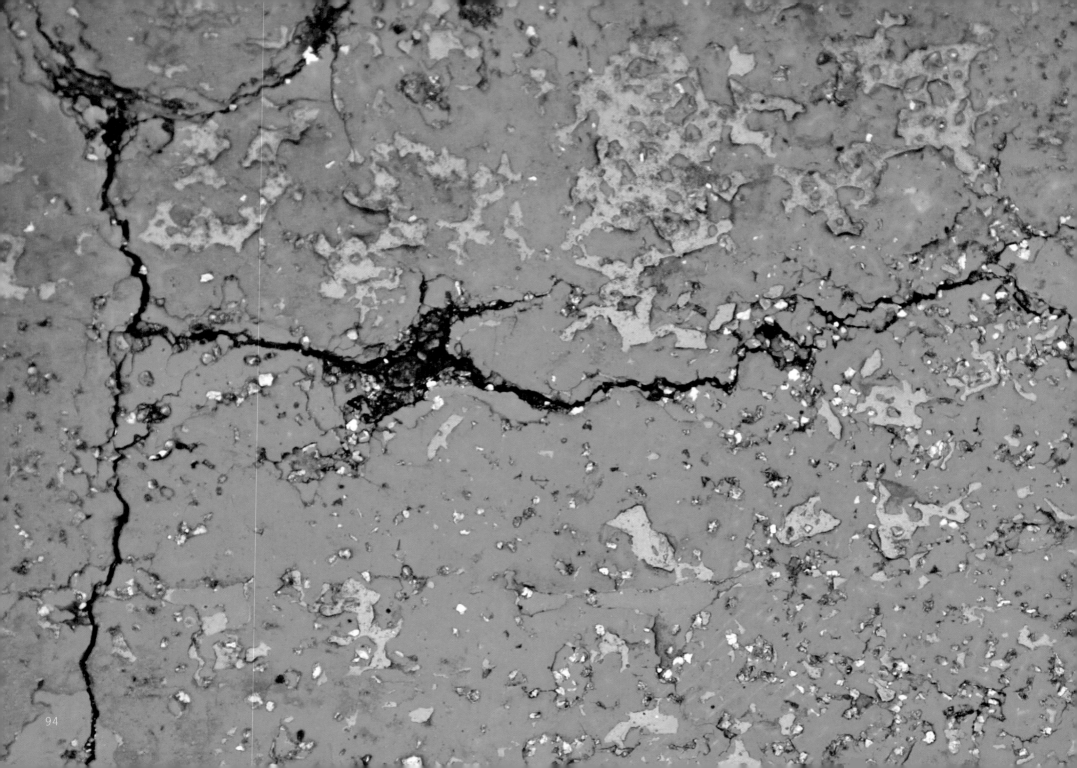

Lush, vibrant, relaxing, and hopeful, green is the color that is most prevalent in the world around us and the color to which the human eye is most attuned. It is the color of nature, of growth and vitality, and of spring. Since the beginning of time it has been used to represent the very essence of life, from the earliest dyes made from malachite and verdigris, emerald, and green earth. Ever since then, thousands of shades and hues of green have colored our world—in art and literature, fashion and culture, as well as our backyards.

Green has always played its part in interiors due to its flexible and restful qualities. The German poet and philosopher Goethe declared it the most restful color and perfect for bedrooms, and many have taken his advice. But green and citrus should not just be confined to bedrooms and, likewise, green should not be assumed only to be contemplative and relaxing. Chartreuse and acacia can make a space dazzle with vivacity; lime and apple bring a sparkling promise of spring to your home; emerald and moss tones can add depth and character to any room. Green can be earthy or glamorous, lively and vivid, or soulful and calm. Its ability to add balance and harmony to a space is one of its major characteristics. Just as the stems and leaves in a backyard are green, no matter what color the flower, a shade of green is the perfect partner to any color and can be used as a neutral to balance other colors, allowing them to sing.

The rooms on the following pages exemplify green's versatility and its innate ability to bring in the world around us.

On pages 98–99, a simple palette of vivid lettuce green and fresh white forms the basis of the room, reflecting the backyard outside. A silky dove-gray rug provides a foothold on which an antique upholstered daybed rests. A sparkling apple and white tie-dye banner filters the sunlight, the same design picked up again as a throw on the bed. To add to the air of nonchalant charm, the bed is strewn with pillows in different shapes and sizes—tweedy washed linens and a large bolster in pale jade strike a note of indulgent relaxation. A pair of vintage armchairs covered in the same linen tweed punctuates the room and adds vitality and modernity.

In the study on pages 103–5, green takes on a new spirit. Two walls are covered in a shaded paper that starts at its base in a rich moss green then fades to acacia and onward to white. The effect is as dramatic as it is restful, drawing one's eye upward to the light and filling the room with a resonant note of moss green. The floor retains its stripped-wood bareness, allowing the walls and the drape at the window to imbue the room with color. To balance this strength, a rich flannel gray is used on the gently curved sofa, its seat upholstered in a mossy-green wool. Dark wood furniture grounds the room and bentwood chairs with their curvy arms add another dimension. Flashes of brilliant alchemilla and mimosa in the form of tall organic vases add a dynamic shot to what is otherwise a sedate, masculine space.

The country bedroom on pages 106–7 shows chartreuse green and acacia in a refined mood. The walls are papered in a monochrome trail of repeating flowers and leaves, which forms the basis of the scheme. A French country bed is painted in a smart lead gray, anchoring the space. The window is dressed with a banner of black-and-white linen stripes that continues the monochrome mood but is partnered at the other side of the window with a vivid chartreuse silk, printed with black-and-white birds and flowers. The vibrant citrus shade also covers the back of a small vintage sofa at the end of the bed; the seat is monochrome stripes. The bed is dressed with vibrant silk stripes of black and white, acacia and lime. The citrus shades give the room a vivacity and glamour; partnered with the formal tailoring of monochrome, the effect is one of refinement and elegance.

In the reception room, featured on pages 110–11, the boundary between the room and the verdant lush backyard beyond is blurred by the strong emerald green that forms the backbone of the decoration. The architecture of the space is powerful, with high ceilings and ornate lintels, demanding a rich tone that will complement and enhance its features. The walls are covered in an almost iridescent emerald-green paper with a geometric detail in graphite that positively glows with vitality. A group of furniture in the center of the room allows other textures to add their own qualities to the mix: a pair of tall, modern wing sofas are upholstered in an intricate velvet in graphite with small spots of chartreuse, lime, and emerald threads reminiscent of a radiant stained-glass window; a rich velvet in dazzling peridot covers the back and picks out the button details. Balancing the vibrant green is a pair of armchairs, one in a warm persimmon, the other in a vivid cobalt blue, giving the scheme a dynamic spirit. Bottle-green vases carry languid stems of white and orange flowers; embellished turquoise pillows and a cobalt-blue lampshade lift the room and give a sharper focus to its exotic richness. There is no doubt that this green space is full of life, but it is the combination of shades and textures that give it a unique character and spirit.

The living room on pages 112–15 finds green in an altogether different mood. Here a warm sage green is paired with tailored black and white, providing the accent of color in an otherwise monochrome scheme. One wall is covered in a paper of overlapping graphite circles on white—an almost hypnotic pattern that is repeated as a drape at the window. Just visible underneath is another drape of glossy silk stripes in black, white, lemon, and lime, giving the room an unexpected shot of zesty color. A rug in shades from forest through to leaf green anchors the room and provides a focal point. Next to it, a charcoal gray sofa adds a restrained, almost serious note while a pair of vintage armchairs in a mix of textures and patterns counters the gravity and adds a note of wit and humor.

Soft citrus green takes on a more reticent role in the morning room on pages 118–21. Here, as it unites a scheme of rich ocher, peony, natural, and carmine, this pale shade is the neutral that gives the space its restful calm. Almost hiding within the exuberance of the large-scale flowered print that covers one wall, hanging in heavy drapes at the window, this dreamy soft green underpins the space with subtlety. The rich tapestry-like floral is repeated on the rug, while a pair of smooth sofas covered in linen stripes of moss, citrus, and natural give the room an expanse of tranquillity and allow the colored flowers to sing out. A small armchair in zesty acacia gives the space the necessary shot of strength, while the overall effect is one of romance and elegance. This particular shade of soft citrus green works with all the colors in the room, allowing them to play their part. It remains firmly in the background—subtle, almost imperceptible, but without it the room would not have the spirit and life that it does.

GREEN
ACACIA
CHARTREUSE
CITRUS
EMERALD
APPLE
MOSS
VERDIGRIS

SIMPLE COLORS
CAN AFFECT THE
INTIMATE FEELINGS
WITH ALL THE MORE
FORCE BECAUSE
THEY ARE SIMPLE.

HENRI MATISSE

I FOUND I COULD SAY THINGS WITH COLOR AND SHAPES THAT
I COULDN'T SAY ANY OTHER WAY—THINGS I HAD NO WORDS FOR.
GEORGIA O'KEEFFE

GREEN IS THE PRIME COLOR OF THE WORLD, AND THAT FROM WHICH ITS LOVELINESS ARISES.

PEDRO CALDERÓN DE LA BARCA

Few colors evoke such an immediate and often divided opinion as pink. For those that love it, it is seen as the color of enduring love and romance, a joyful, positive color, feminine, gentler in its sensuality than red, yet no less powerful. But this is only part of the story: pink, while undoubtedly all of these things, is so much more.

Shocking pink is the definitive color when one wants to make an impact: suddenly that femininity finds dynamism and a confidence that cannot be ignored. Powerful and sassy, shocking pink is perhaps femininity in its most strident form, yet this seemingly unforgettable, hard-to-ignore color melds into the background as a type of uniform in the great subcontinent of India, where it is ubiquitous and worn by men and women alike. In Jaipur, the famous Pink City, the houses, forts, and palaces are painted a soft shell pink to suffuse the glare of the sun's rays and symbolize a warm welcome. In the rest of Rajasthan, where it is seen as a color of importance and occasion, men wear pink turbans to celebrate weddings and major celebrations.

In Argentina, the soft plaster-pink of the Casa Rosada or Pink Palace is the country's seat of power—a striking and resonant symbol of authority and control. To Luis Barragán, the celebrated Mexican architect, a bright fuchsia pink was integral to his signature style; a striking pink wall brought a joyful definition to his own special brand of modernity and blurred the lines between the minimalism of concrete and soulful expression.

Pink often seems to elicit a sensual response. After bleak winters, the first blooms of cherry blossoms in the spring—those dark branches laden with an abundance of pink petals —make one's heart sing. Similarly, the intoxicating fragrance of summer peonies, from the palest blush to the deepest velvety magenta, reminds us of nature's extraordinary ability to create a palette like no other.

In an interior space, pink in all its forms can add a vivacious feminine flourish. Used in a modern way, it can soften hard, graphic lines or inject a pop of exuberance, while in traditional rooms it can be nostalgic, elegant, and classical.

In the beautiful sun-filled living room on pages 128–31 a vibrant cerise pink is used with crisp white to create a relaxed, gentle mood. The walls are papered in a design redolent of traditional Japanese calligraphy with exquisitely drawn branches and flowers colored in with watery washes of blossom pink. Against the serenity of the walls and drapes, an elegant button-back sofa is upholstered in a heavy white linen, its buttons of magenta tweed adding definition to its shape. The same rich tweed is used to cover a fluted armchair, adding a punch of power to the softness of the scheme.

The palette is kept tight and simple but the mix of textures and shapes gives the room a more eclectic feel—graphic checks of magenta, white, and charcoal used on the backs of chairs add an unexpected lively touch. The room is anchored with a charcoal rug that relates back to the branches on the walls and drapes, while simple striped and checked pillows invite one to curl up and relax. Here pink is both strong and gentle; making a statement while providing an elegant backdrop.

On pages 132–3, a detail of an ornate drawing room shows pink in a restrained mood. The architecture is classical and elegant with plaster moldings and high ceilings. A digitally printed wallpaper of sepia dahlias—some highlighted in blossom, mauve, persimmon, and magenta—strikes an unexpected note within the carved panels; the sepia tone and the photographic quality of the flowers nod to the classical references in the room while the lively flowers set a different pace, giving the room an insouciance that plays with the mood. A contemporary Henry Bertoia chair further shifts the balance and a reading light with its edgy cord in bright pink—its shade revealing an equally bright interior—adds touches of color and wit. The large sofa in blossom-pink washed velvet adds a luxurious twist, with one crimson-and-linen-striped pillow providing strength and definition.

The morning room on pages 136–9 shows how magenta pink can be both elegant and contemporary. The flowered paper, with its artfully repeating studies of pavonia blooms in fuchsia, citrus, and monochrome with dark forest-green leaves, sets the tone of tailored romance. An exuberant multicolored flowered drape hangs at the recessed window, its boldness countered by a washed linen stripe of sage and white. An unlined heavy silk banner dresses another window in hot pink, olive, and persimmon stripes while a pair of cool, generous sofas in heavy white linen balances the strength of colors and provides a light focal point. The sofas, with their smart, cobalt blue stitch detailing, sit on layered rugs: one of hot pink flowers and the other a geometric monochrome Berber, each balancing the color and neutrals in the room, the geometric stripes tailoring the exuberance of the flowers. A vintage chair in deep turquoise instantly cools the heat of the pink, while subtle touches of flat gray—a linen pillow on the sofa or a seat cover in graphite—stop the room being overly sweet and feminine.

The large bedroom on pages 140–41 finds pink at its vibrant, sassy, and confident best. A simple palette of magenta and white proves to be unashamedly feminine and edgy at the same time. Crisp white linen covers the bed while a tie-dyed throw of shocking pink and pillows of different shapes and sizes add texture and a dynamic touch. The graphic black lines of the four-poster bed add definition and modernity that is counterbalanced by the pure white sheer linen hanging from the bed.

The adjoining sitting room (pages 142–5) uses the stunning partnership of magenta and white as a base to which other colors and textures are added. The same tie-dye dresses one window with a fall of magenta and white while at another window a pure linen, shading from hot peony pink through blossom and eventually to white, filters the light. The third window is hung with a cascade of sharp, acid green and white linen—the color mirroring the intensity of the pink but cooling it; the use of the same tie-dyed language adds a note of continuity and calm to a vibrant scheme. A tailored generous sofa grounds the room, its seat covered in the rich magenta, while the pillows in a heavier version of the shaded drape draw the eye upward to the soaring ceilings. Simple yet luxurious white rugs pull the whole room together and an antique bench with slim peppermint pillows adds a soft, cool breath to balance the intensity of the hot pink. A vintage chair with graduated lilac linen cover and a casual pale jade throw provide further stillness to the room.

In the study on pages 146–9, pink is used as one note in a symphony of colors. It is by no means the dominant force, but rather an intrinsic element showing that bright pink can be a team player, not merely the hero in an interior. Here a paper of large bouquets of flowers in cobalt, orange, alchemilla, and hot pink color one wall and the same pattern on tumbled white linen hangs at the open French doors.

The complexity of the design is matched in intensity with a textured round rug of cobalt blue on which rests a slim chaise of the same shade. Its gently curving back is covered in a bright mango felt that one can glimpse from different angles. The exuberance of the flowers is given a graphic edge with a tailored banner and pillows of ultramarine and white silk stripes. A solitary pillow of citrus on another cobalt blue armchair adds that jolt of freshness to the intoxicating mix. The study leads to a garden room, where the same scheme continues, though now with a touch more hot pink among the leafy fronds of the exotic plants.

PINK
BLUSH
ROSE MADDER LAKE
BLOSSOM
MAGENTA
ROSE
CERISE
PEONY

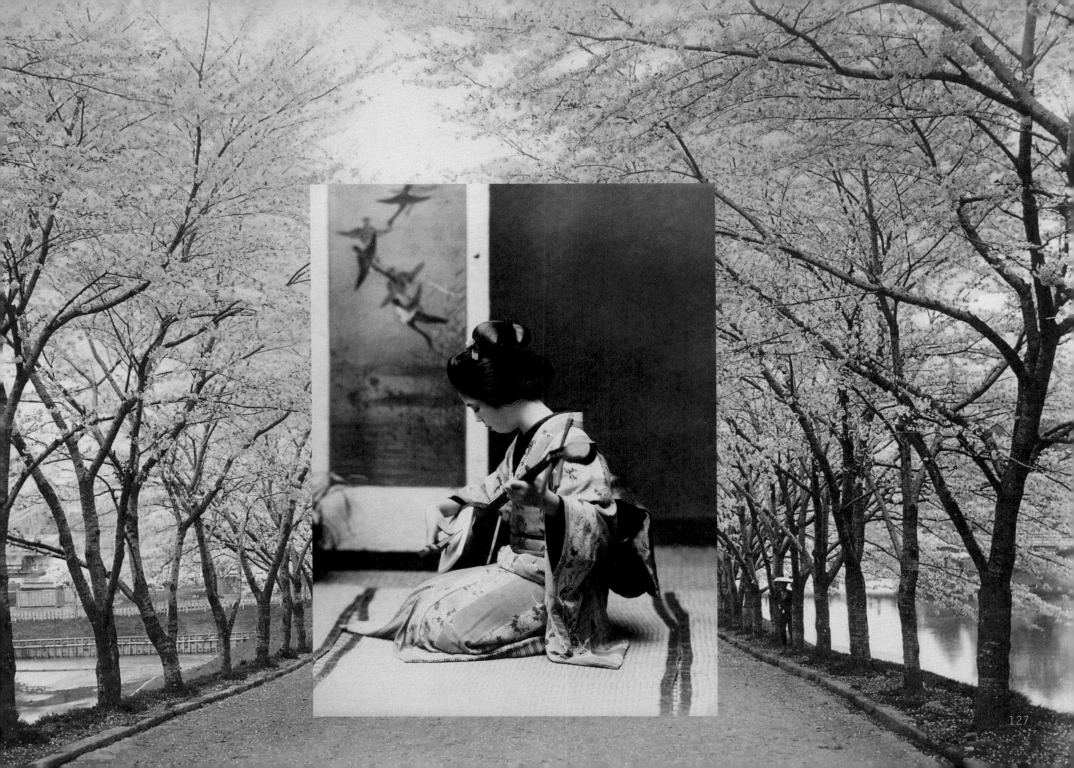

131

NEVER DULL

FRESH

DELICATE

BEAUTIFUL

VIBRANT

PINK

SHOCKING

SUBTLE

EXQUISITE

137

ACID
GREEN
AND
MAGENTA
PURE
COLOR
GLOWING
WITH
LIGHT

THE CRAVING FOR COLOR IS A NATURAL
NECESSITY JUST AS FOR WATER AND
FIRE. COLOR IS A RAW MATERIAL
INDISPENSABLE TO LIFE.
AT EVERY ERA OF HIS EXISTENCE
AND HIS HISTORY, THE HUMAN BEING
HAS ASSOCIATED COLOR WITH
HIS JOYS, HIS ACTIONS,
AND HIS PLEASURES.
FERNAND LÉGER

Halfway between blue and red lies the color purple. Warm, rich, luxurious, and powerful, purple has a magical, mysterious quality, in all its corresponding shades. Historically, it has been seen as the color of wealth, wisdom, and spirituality. The color is as old as the lavender, lilac, violet, and heliotrope plants that have colored our backyards for thousands of years. In the eighteenth century BCE, the Minoans pioneeered the extraction of purple dye from tropical sea snails. Legend has it that the dye was first discovered by the god Heracles, who noticed that his dog's mouth was stained purple after eating the snails. His companion, the beautiful nymph Tyrus, said she would only stay with Heracles if he made her a cloak of the same color; he duly did and the color Tyrian purple was born. The dye and the cloth made from it became so famous that the Greeks called the land Phoenicia, or Purple Land.

Purple was the first color to be made synthetically in 1856—a shade called Mauveine, created from coal tar. One of the most famous mauve rooms in the world is in the Alexander Palace, near St. Petersburg, in Russia, where the Tsarina Alexandra commissioned a silk from Paris to match a sprig of lilac that her husband had given her. The vivid hue covered the walls and furniture and even hung at the enormous windows. For many years it was the most celebrated room in Russia and it is still the room that most fascinates the visiting public.

Today, purple retains its air of nobility and splendor, but has also gained a following among modernists, who use it for its impact and depth. Yet it is the softer shades of this family that have been used most in interiors. In the rooms that follow, purple is shown in all its guises, from deepest violet to the softest lilac—each depicting the distinctive mood of contemplation and sophistication that comes with a dash of purple.

The formal living room on pages 154–57 shows rich cardinal purple at its sophisticated best. The proportions of the room are grand, with high ceilings and wood paneling in a pale gray. Oak parquet flooring and a large marble fireplace further heighten the traditional mood, and the classical painting above the fireplace dictates the style of the room—demanding a richness and gravitas equal to its own weighty importance. Various panels in the room are covered in a theatrical wallpaper, featuring antique urns bursting with roses, damson-colored tulips, and citrus dahlias on a dark graphite background. A larger version of the pattern hangs at the windows, where it is heavily trimmed with a deep olive fringe. Both

the depth of color and the urn design nod to classicism. And just visible, next to the heavy drape, another banner of dazzling magenta and citrus stripes adds a sharper note and a dynamic flourish. The floor is anchored with a warm magenta rug in a large-scale animal motif. A chaise longue is covered in a grape version of the rug's design, its elegant arm in stripes of mulberry and damson silk lifting the scheme. A lampshade of similar silk stripe is edged with a glamorous beaded trim, adding a further light touch to the resonant damson and magenta. A sumptuous armchair, covered in luxurious damson, grape, and mulberry striped velvet, echoes the colors of the flowers on the wall and at the window. And a single pillow edged in singing turquoise somehow cuts the richness of the room. The scheme is a study in balance: rich color against sharp, modern dynamic touches in a traditional setting.

The intimate living room on pages 158–59 moves the richness of purple into an altogether lighter mood—a rich violet being used as an accent rather than the key player. The walls are papered in a cool gray, faux-stone effect, which effortlessly works off the bleached wood floors. The elegant buttoned sofa covered in a smart geometric linen in white and natural, its seat in a heavy, stone-colored linen, continues the neutral scheme. Color makes its entrance at a pair of tall, arched windows: one is dressed in a heavy linen printed with expansive hydrangeas in warm rose pink (its foliage a stronger graphite), the other in a rich silk stripe of violet, blackberry, and damson that brings a feeling of warmth and weight to the lightness of the room. A pair of silky eggplant rugs grounds the room further and a small vintage chair unites the contrasting lightness and weight with its silvery gray seat and rich, dappled purple back. The room is both light and rich—purple plays its part to perfection.

Rich berry tones are one part of a sophisticated mix of dynamic colors in the morning room on pages 160–61. The walls are covered in a shaded paper that starts at deep violet and fades through to a softer cyclamen and onward to white, gradually drawing the eye upward but depicting the stillness of one color despite its gradual movement. At a tall arched window hangs a painterly explosion of printed flowers in shades of amethyst, damson, cobalt, and lime. Among the riot of colors, some of the flowers are depicted in graphic black and white, balancing the pace of the print. The shaded design on the walls appears again as an unlined banner next to the flowers, keeping the balance light, while at an adjoining window the print is repeated, this time alongside a heavy fall of silky stripes, in cobalt, damson, forest green, and monochrome. The lush, grape-velvet sofa is both strong and elegant, anchoring the vivacity of the flowers and adding drama and weight. Rugs of dove gray and cool turquoise layer the floor and the same singing turquoise colors pillows, seat backs, and glass vases. These touches lighten the richness and stop the room feeling cloying or heavy. In the hallway leading to the room (pages 162–63), a central stool of damson velvet and monochrome stripes, finished with a deep alchemilla fringe, offers a glimpse of the drama ahead.

In the suite of rooms on pages 166–69 it is a softer shade of purple that helps create a light, dancing vivacity. In the hallway, a vibrant pattern of tumbling flowers in soft, chalky shades of lilac, minty jade, and palest ocher covers the walls and sets a romantic tone. In the living room beyond, the flowered pattern of the walls in the hallway dresses a tall pair of windows with its dancing flowers. Here, a cool pale jade, used on large angular sofas in shaded linen and a vintage armchair in plush textured velvet, counterbalances the soft wisteria color. Rugs in the softest aqua preserve the lightness of touch and the chalky heathery purple provides accents of warmth and depth.

In the pair of bedrooms on pages 172–73 and 174–75, the softest lilac is used in a variety of ways to produce a dreamy, contemplative spirit. In the first, drapes of delicate mauve flowers printed on glittering white silk banners make for a supremely feminine feel. This prettiness is balanced, and a tailored element introduced to the room, by a dynamic tie-dyed fall of dove-gray and white linen at one window and a striped silk banner of alchemilla and mauve at the other. The air of romance prevails though, with delicately flocked walls of lilac velvet, a mauve gray rug, and an upholstered French bed scattered with wisteria-colored throws and pillows. Two curvy chairs complete the setting, their seats and backs covered in chalky pale moss and pale mauve, with animal-skin velvet, in pale lilac and black, giving the room an unexpected dash of modernity. The result is a room that is supremely pretty without being sweet.

In the second bedroom the walls are papered in a watery mauve damask, and a shaded linen canopy in heather provides a cloud-like dreaminess above the bed. The softness is balanced with crisp textures—washed linen stripes of mauve, heather, black, and white dress the bolsters and pillows on the bed, and a vintage chair covered in a crisp, utilitarian check of mauve, black, and white gives the room a tailored finish.

PURPLE
LAVENDER
HELIOTROPE
VIOLET
ORCHID
MAUVE
PANSY
HEATHER

RICH
VIOLET
AND
PLUM
ANCHOR
A COOL
NEUTRAL
ROOM

ORCHID
MALLOW
WISTERIA
LILAC
ROMANTIC
SUBTLE
SERENE
ETHEREAL

SMOKY MAUVE

UNDERSTATED

SILVER

LAVENDER

GRAY

DUSKY

ROSE PINK

BY LAW, ALL BUILDINGS SHOULD BE WHITE.

LE CORBUSIER

"White is not a mere absence of color; it is a shining and affirmative thing, as fierce as red, as definite as black. God paints in many colors; but He never paints so gorgeously, I had almost said so gaudily, as when He paints in white." So wrote the philosopher and poet G. K. Chesterton. It is an interesting observation that, while it can be seen as an absence of color, white is very much a color with its own characteristics and personality. It is the color of purity, innocence, and clean slates; it is the color of beginnings, of light, cleanliness, and clarity. In the West it is the color of choice for brides, whereas in the Far East it is the color most associated with mourning. It is the color of peace, of truce, and of surrender; it is also the color of perfection and simplicity. In so many ways it is shining and affirmative, saying "yes" to a myriad of possibilities. White surrounds us in a way no other color can and it is the default color for many of us when it comes to choice; for if we are not sure, then apparently ... we choose white. But as easy as it may seem, white or natural is not always easy to decorate with. It can be bland and lifeless, cold and sterile; too many underlying shades of neutral can render a space dull and boring. One must have an understanding of what these tones need to ensure they are none of the above, but rather dynamic and interesting.

On the pages that follow, there are rooms that show how white and natural can make a space sing with shining clarity and how they can echo natural surfaces and create calm spaces that have both personality and vivacity.

On pages 182–93, shades of white and alabaster are used to accentuate the crisp lines of a contemporary family home. The house is uncompromisingly modern, but it also features age-old techniques that give it a rich character. Dry-stone walling has been used on many of the external walls and they can be glimpsed from the acres of glass doors that line the rooms of the house. The house has a natural warmth, sitting as it does in a south-facing dip in a valley,

surrounded by hills and countryside. The floors are concrete and many of the walls are whitened cast concrete; light floods in from glass slices in the ceilings. Here, texture is key. The palette is kept to tones of natural and white, while texture and subtle mixes of pattern create a lively, inviting space. A slim, almost floating, white leather bench sets the tone as you enter. Simple, chic, and as striking as the architecture, it is decorated with one alabaster linen pillow that is decoratively trimmed with frayed silk. The play on textures begins. In the main wing of the living space, a large modular sofa in white leather defines a casual entertaining space. A pair of large rugs of chalk and pumice stripes further grounds the space and adds another layer of texture to the stone, concrete, and glass. Piles of pillows artfully arranged on the sofa introduce new notes of houndstooth linen and striped silk in snowy white, smoky gray, and ivory. A pair of armchairs, with curvy bentwood arms, provides further seating: their covers of off-white velvet and stone linen add to the mix. A vintage table with pearl mosaic tiles and beech legs adds another layer of texture and keeps the palette alive, while a daybed of beech and white linen finishes the space.

At the other end of the room a slim slice of white concrete creates an elegant dining table that is dressed with intricate pieces of chalky white ceramic, their complex moldings adding further subtle twists to the atmosphere of the room. An organic, raw-looking wooden console table houses a collection of white porcelain figures, adding a note of humor and wit to the otherwise restrained room. Simple curvy glassware holds elegant stems of asparagus fern and white star-of-Bethlehem flowers—their greenness nodding to the countryside beyond the glass and adding a note of color. The layers of texture and harmonious shades of white and off-white, plaster and alabaster create a calm and beautiful space but one that sings with personality and individuality. At the far end of the living room, a small vestibule continues the atmosphere: organic, raw wooden benches sit on concrete floors next to white concrete walls. Simple, printed cotton pillows add pattern to the texture and soften the almost monastic serenity of the space.

In a bedroom of the same house, on pages 194–97, a silvery metallic paper of trailing flowers evokes a dreamy sensitivity that is both contemporary and romantic. The delicate flowers are subtle and almost classical, yet the soft, shimmery ground of the paper gives them a glamorous, contemporary note in this modern, country bedroom. A vintage teal rug adds warmth and depth to the space; another wooden console table holds more treasures. The mix of organic textures—like wood, glass, and stone—restrains the gaiety of the flowers, and a simple upholstered armchair in chalk linen and oyster velvet further tailors the femininity, striking a note of modernity and simplicity.

Smoky gray is the starting point for a small but elegant study on pages 200–201. The cue is taken from the stone moldings and limestone lintels of the doorways and fireplace, which give the space a sense of character. The walls are papered in a dove gray that is embellished with tiny reflective beads arranged in lace-like patterns. At the window hangs an unlined banner of tie-dyed linen, in charcoal and dove gray, that softly filters the sunlight. The effect is one of sparkling subtlety, serious with just a touch of understated nonchalance.

Gold and silver, or indeed any metallic, can be used with off-white and natural to add texture while remaining true to a neutral spirit. In the detail taken from a living room, on pages 204–5, the walls are papered with a design of golden flowers on an ivory background. The shimmer of the flowers reflects the light and suffuses the space with a sparkling glamour. At the window, a banner of sheer linen flowers, in tones of soft sepia, pearl, and lead, is trimmed with an extravagant fringe of charcoal that gives a stroke of definition to the room.

WHITE
ALABASTER
NATURAL
CHALK
ECRU
STONE
SMOKE
PEBBLE

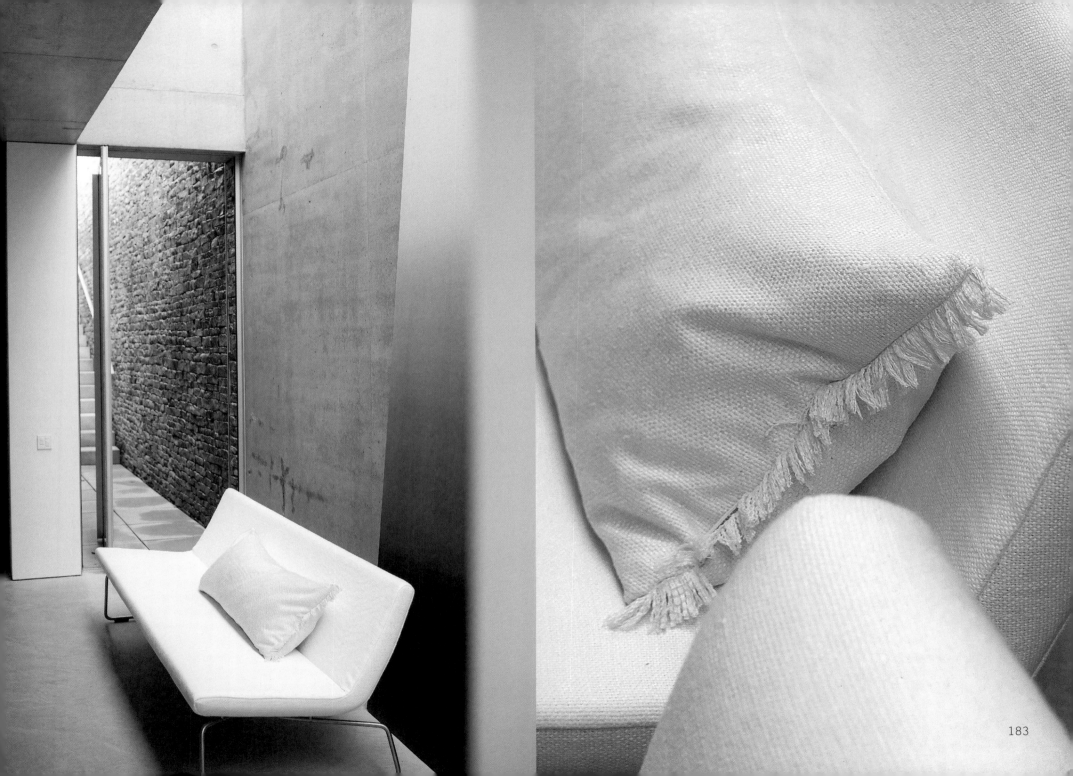

SUBTLE
NATURAL
CALM
HARMONIOUS
STONE
AND
EARTH
ALLOW SUBTLE
TEXTURES
CENTER STAGE

DELICATE

DOVE

SHINGLE

ALABASTER

IVORY

SUBTLE

ELEGANT

SOPHISTICATED

TEXTURED

PLASTER

DRIFTWOOD

MARBLE

STONE

FADED

ELEGANCE

PATINA

DESIGNERS GUILD RETAILERS

DesignersGuildBed,BathandAccessoriesaredistributedthroughouttheUnitedStatesandCanadabyDesignersGuildInc.,Suite1903,230FifthAvenue,NewYorkCity,NY10001.Tel:2129674540. To find your local retailer, please visit www.designersguild.com/stockists

DesignersGuildFabricandWallpapersaredistributedinDesignandDecorationBuildingsthroughouttheUnitedStatesandCanadabyOsborne&LittleInc.,90CommerceRoad,Stamford,CT06902. Tel: 203 359 1500. They are also available through the following showrooms:

CANADA

ALBERTA
DWA Showroom
501–536 Avenue S.E.
Calgary T2G 1W5
403-245-4014

ONTARIO
Primavera
160 Pears Avenue, Suite 110
Toronto M5R 3P8
416-921-3334

USA

ARIZONA
Dean-Warren
2716 N. 68th Street
Suite One
Scottsdale 85257
480-990-9233

CALIFORNIA
Osborne & Little Inc.
Pacific Design Center, Suite B643
8687 Melrose Avenue
Los Angeles 90069
310-659-7667

Osborne & Little Inc.
101 Henry Adams Street, Suite 435
San Francisco 94103
415-255-8987

COLORADO
Shanahan Collection
Denver Design District
595 S. Broadway, Suite 105W
Denver 80209
303-778-7088

CONNECTICUT
Osborne & Little Inc.
90 Commerce Road
Stamford 06902
203-359-1500

DISTRICT OF COLOMBIA
Osborne & Little Inc.
300 D Street S.W., Suite 435
Washington 20024
202-554-8800

FLORIDA
Ammon Hickson Inc.
1855 Griffin Road, Suite B-364
Dania Beach
Florida 33004
954-925-1555

GEORGIA
Grizzel & Mann Inc.
351 Peachtree Hills Avenue N.E., Suite 120
Atlanta 30305
404-261-5932

ILLINOIS
Osborne & Little Inc.
Merchandise Mart, Suite 610
Chicago 60654
312-467-0913

KANSAS
Designers Only
5225 W. 75th Street
Prairie Village 60628
913-649-3778

MASSACHUSETTS
Osborne & Little Inc.
The Boston Design Center, Suite 551
Boston 02210
617-737-2927

MINNESOTA
Scherping Westphal
International Market Square
275 Market Street, Suite 209
Minneapolis 55405
612-822-2700

MISSOURI
Design & Detail
2731 Sutton Boulevard, Suite 100
Maplewood 63143
314-781-3336

NEW YORK
Designers Guild Inc.
Suite 1903, 230 Fifth Avenue
New York City
NY 10001
212-967-4540

Osborne & Little Inc.
979 Third Avenue, Suite 520
New York 10022
212-751-3333

OHIO
Gregory Alonso Inc.
Ohio Design Center
23533 Mercantile Road, Suite 113
Beachwood 44122

PENNSYLVANIA
JW Showroom Inc.
The Marketplace, Suite 304
2400 Market Street
Philadelphia 19103
215-561-2270

TEXAS
I.D Collection
1025 N. Stemmons Frwy, Suite 745
Dallas 75207
214-698-0226

I.D Collection
5120 Woodway Drive, Suite 4001
Houston 77056
713-623-2344

WASHINGTON
The Dixon Group Inc.
The Seattle Design Center 5701
6th Avenue South, Plaza Suite 162
Seattle 98108
206-767-4454

Designers Guild products are available in
over 80 countries around the world. For full
details on all of our agents and distributors
worldwide please visit our website
www.designersguild.com

CENTRAL & SOUTH
AMERICA

ARGENTINA   Miranda Green
DOMINICAN REPUBLIC   Casa Kyrez
BRAZIL   Beraldin Textiles

CHILE   Importaciones Santa Cuz Limitada
COLOMBIA   Denise Webb Textiles
ECUADOR   Home Identity
MEXICO   Artell
PANAMA   Metropolitan Furniture S.A.
PERU   Romantex S.A.
URUGUAY   Nicole Hernstadt
VENEZUELA   Idea 58 C.A.

EUROPE
AUSTRIA   Designers Guild
BELGIUM   Alinee
CYPRUS   Loizoudi
DENMARK   Zenout
FINLAND   Oy Vallila Interior
FRANCE   Designers Guild
GERMANY   Designers Guild
GREECE   Eurotextile
ITALY   Designers Guild
MALTA   Design House
NETHERLANDS   Wilhelmine Van
   Aerssen Agenturen
NORWAY   Riis Interiør
PORTUGAL   Pedroso & Osório
SPAIN   Designers Guild
SWEDEN   Designers Guild
SWITZERLAND   Nadine Braun
TURKEY   Homteks

AUSTRALASIA
AUSTRALIA   Radford Furnishings
NEW ZEALAND   Icon Textiles Ltd.

FAR EAST
CHINA   Yada Tissu
HONG KONG   Avant Garde Designs
INDONESIA   Pacific Hues Indonesia
JAPAN   Designers Guild
KOREA   Sedec
MALAYSIA   Janine
PHILIPPINES   Rubeni Corp
SINGAPORE   Romanez
TAIWAN   Andari Group
THAILAND   Charoen Decor International

INDIA   Floor & Furnishings

MIDDLE EAST
ISRAEL   Illith
MIDDLE EAST (except Israel)   Maison D'Art

AFRICA
SOUTH AFRICA   Home Fabrics
MOROCCO   Rodesma
EYGPT   Maison D'Art

ACKNOWLEDGMENTS

Special thanks to: Amanda Back for her sensitive and thoughtful words; Jo Willer and Blythe Bruckner for their creativity and support; my wonderful and talented team at Designers Guild – too great in number to mention individually, but heartfelt thanks for all their hard work, support and commitment; Meryl Lloyd for her fantastic eye; James Merrell for his extraordinary photographs; Anne Furniss, our brilliant editor, and the team at Quadrille for all their encouragement.

The publishers would like to thank the following for their permission to reproduce images in this book. Every effort has been made to trace the photographers and copyright holders and we apologise for any unintentional omission. We would be pleased to insert the appropriate acknowledgement in any subsequent edition.

All photographs by James Merrell except the following pages:
1 Nicolas Vasse; **4, 98** Natalee Hazelwood/Alamy; **8-9** Hannes Kilian; **14** © Edwin Giesbers/naturepl.com; **15** Infanta Catalina Micaela, Duchess of Savoy (1567-97), daughter of Philip II of Spain (1556-98) and Isabella of Valois (1545-68), married Charles Emmanuel, Duke of Savoy, 1585, Anguissola, Sofonisba (c.1532-1625)/ Prado, Madrid, Spain/The Bridgeman Art Library; **18 left** © The Trustees of the British Museum; **18 right** Blue Ruin 1; **20** © Tammy Hanratty/ Corbis; **21** Ilona Wellmann © Trevillion Images; **24** (left) Målning av Urban Målare, 1535 (Photo: Stockholms Stadsmuseum); **26, 36, 68 left, 90, 94, 116, 117, 122 left, 123 left, 135, 151 right, 165, 178, 179, 198, 199** Getty Images; **27** Vilhelm Hammershøi "Sunbeams or Sunlight", Ordrupgaard; **31** Girl in Japanese Costume, c.1888 (oil on canvas), Chase, William Merritt (1849-1916) Brooklyn Museum of Art, New York,

USA/Gift of Isabella S. Kurtz in memory of Charles M. Kurtz/The Bridgeman Art Library; **37, 146 centre, 150 left, 160 left, 202** Tricia Guild (apart from below left James Merrell), **203** Tricia Guild; **40** left Portrait of a Woman (oil on canvas) (detail) (see 164366, 164367, 164368), Winterhalter, Franz Xaver (1806-73) (circle of) Musée des Beaux-Arts, Carcassonne, France/ Patrice Cartier/The Bridgeman Art Library; **47** Nature Picture Library/ Alamy; **54** left, sunrise-art.com; **54** right Gregory M Zenitsky; **58** Eureka/ Alamy; **59** Portrait of a Woman (oil on canvas) (detail) (see 164366, 164367, 164369), Winterhalter, Franz Xaver (1806-73) (circle of) Musée des Beaux-Arts, Carcassonne, France/Patrice Cartier/The Bridgeman Art Library; **68** right Portrait of Sarah Eleonor Fermor (1740-1824) 1749-50 (oil on canvas), Vishnyakov, Ivan Yakovlevich (1699-1761) State Russian Museum, St. Petersburg, Russia/Giraudon/ The Bridgeman Art Library; **69 left** © Jonathan Buckley/http://www. flowerphotos.com/Eye Ubiquitous/ Corbis; **69 right** Michael Levy; **72** © Richard Cummins/Corbis; **73** Clouds shadow in sea water (photo)/Republic of Maldives/Dinodia/The Bridgeman Art Library; **80 centre** © George D. Lepp/ Corbis; **82** Adrian van Leen; **83** Lip Kee Yap; **88** right Woman with a Fan, 1871 (pencil & w/c on paper), Watson, John Dawson (1832-92) Private Collection/Photo © The Maas Gallery,

London/The Bridgeman Art Library; **91** Pat Canova/Alamy; **93** right Gardens OnLine; **95** Detail of front light of a lime green customised vintage hotrod car, Las Vegas, USA/PYMCA/UIG/ The Bridgeman Art Library; **100** Chris Hellier/Alamy; **101** © Clive Nichols/ Corbis; **102** Kokay Szabolcs; **108** left Chinh Hoang; **108 centre** Elena Nicolajeva/Alamy; **108 right** © Fritz von der Schulenburg/Interior Archive/ Arcaid/Corbis; **109** David Ross; **110 left** © Charles Smith/Corbis; **122 right** Photograph courtesy of Sotheby's Inc. © 2009; 126-127 Photography Collection, Miriam and Ira D. Wallach Division of Art, Prints and Photographs, The New York Public Library, Astor, Lenox and Tilden Foundations; **127** © Michael Maslan Historic Photographs/ Corbis; **130** Clare Gainey/Alamy; **131** Radius Images/Alamy; **131 below** Dave Watts /Alamy; **133** "Tohuana de Fiesta", 1937, Photograph by Luis Márquez, Online Image. University of Houston Digital Library http://digital. lib.uh.edu/u?/p15195coll13,6; **134** JTB Media Creation Inc/Alamy; **141 left** Garden World Images; **150 right** © Condé Nast Archive/Corbis; **151 left** © Gillian Plummer/Eye Ubiquitous/ Corbis; **164** thanks to Bronte Austen; **171** Andrew Lewington/Cambrian Caving Council; **176** Uros Petrovic; **177** © VIEW Pictures Ltd/Alamy; **186** Dick Daniels; **187** Miscellaneous Stock/Alamy; **189** centre Daniel Borzynski/Alamy.

First published in the United States of America in 2013 by
Rizzoli International Publications, Inc.
300 Park Avenue South
New York, NY 10010
www.rizzoliusa.com

Originally published in 2013 as Colour Deconstructed in the United Kingdom by
Quadrille Publishing Limited
Alhambra House
27-31 Charing Cross Road
London WC2H 0LS

Editorial Director Anne Furniss
Design Meryl Lloyd
Tricia Guild's Creative Manager Jo Willer
Picture Research Katie Horwich
Copy Editor Zelda Turner
Production James Finan, Vincent Smith
Text © Quadrille Publishing Ltd 2013
Photographs © James Merrell 2013
Design and layout © Quadrille Publishing Ltd 2013

2013 2014 2015 / 10 9 8 7 6 5 4 3 2 1
Printed in China

ISBN: 978-0-8478-4069-4
Library of Congress Catalog Control Number: 2013933347